AF374817

Fifteen Fallacious Reasons Not to Text on the Toilet

Written and Illustrated by

Johnathan Lauris

There is no evidence that texting on the toilet is safe, therefore it must be dangerous.

DANGER

You can poop,

you can text a poop,

but you can't text on the toilet.

Wicked Witch
Roasted Baby
tastes like...
Chocolate Ice Cream?

Texting on the toilet is bad for the environment because it contributes to global warming.

Only people who hate baby pandas text on the toilet.

Do you hate baby pandas?

People who text on the toilet

often lose their phones

to toilet ticklers.

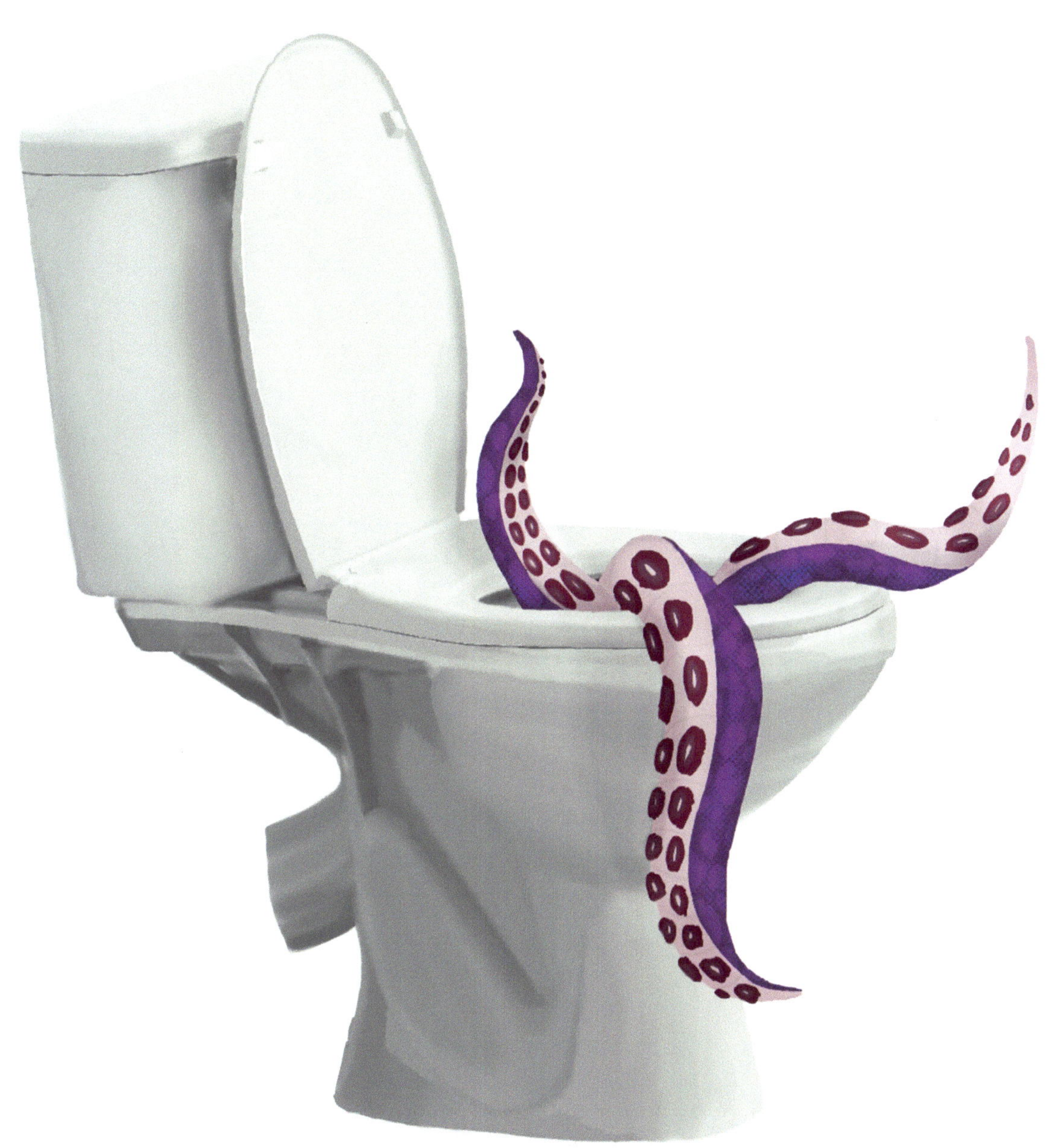

Texting on the toilet is a modern practice that goes against the tradition of reading books while you poop.

The majority of people will tell you
that texting on the toilet can lead to toilet upset.

DON'T DO IT!

You will get pregnant and die!

JUST
SAY
NO!

You can text on the toilet

or you can tell your sphincter monster to go suck a

juice box...

but not both.

Grape Murder
concentrate
100%
NOT
Juice

Texting on the toilet can cause hemorrhoids which can burst leading to Bloodybutt Thruster Disorder (BBTD).

Anyone who thinks it is a good idea to text on the
toilet must have fallen down the stupid tree and hit
every branch on the way.

Texting on the toilet leads to sensory overload and loss of focus resulting in chronic insanity.

This one guy was so busy texting that when he went to
sit down he tripped into the shower curtain and
became a bathroom burrito. But don't worry, you
won't be burritofied if you don't text
on the toilet.

Texting is a way to release information but on the toilet you should only be concerned with releasing waste.

Mobix
0
EXTENDED
PERFORMANCE
EXTRA VIRGIN
OLIVE OIL
0W-40

This book is absurd and filled with logical fallacies you absolutely should not believe. It is totally fine to text on the toilet

... if you accept this isn't a fallacy.

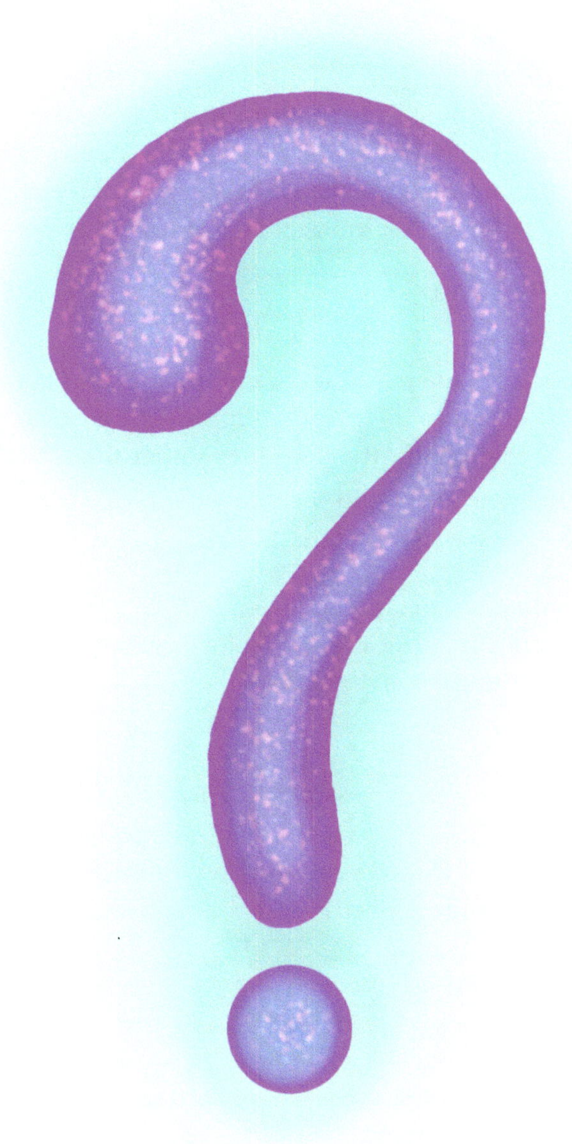

Fallacy Used in Alphabetical Order:

Ad Hominem:
An argument where someone attacks the person making
an argument rather than addressing the argument itself.
It diverts attention from the issue at hand by focusing on
the character, motives, or other attributes of the person
involved.

Ad Populism:
An argument made based on the premise that if many
people believe it to be true, then it must be true. It
appeals to the popularity of an idea rather than
presenting logical reasoning.

Anecdotal Fallacy:
The anecdotal fallacy occurs when people use their
limited personal experience to make sweeping
conclusions about a given topic.

Appeal to Ignorance:
An argument that a proposition is true because it has not
yet been proven false, or that it is false because it has not
yet been proven true. It relies on the absence of evidence
rather than evidence itself.

Appeal to Tradition:
An argument claiming something to be true or better
simply because it is older, traditional, or "has always
been done." It assumes that what is old or traditional is
automatically correct.

Fallacy Used in Alphabetical Order Continued:

Bandwagon Fallacy
An argument that something is true or correct simply
because it is popular or that everyone is doing it.

Circular Reasoning
This fallacy occurs when the conclusion of an argument
is assumed in one of the premises. The argument goes in
a circle and does not provide any actual evidence for the
conclusion.

Equivocation:
This fallacy occurs when a key term or phrase in an
argument is used ambiguously or in multiple senses,
leading to a misleading or false conclusion.

Fallacy Fallacy (Argumentum Ad Logicam)
This is the formal fallacy of analyzing an argument and
inferring that, since it contains a fallacy, its conclusion
must be false.

False Cause (Post Hoc Ergo Propter Hoc)
This fallacy occurs when it is assumed that because one
event followed another, the first event must have caused
the second. It confuses correlation with causation.

False Dilemma (False Dichotomy)
This fallacy occurs when only two options are presented
as the only possible choices when, in fact, other
alternatives may exist. It oversimplifies the situation and
forces a binary choice.

Fallacy Used in Alphabetical Order Continued:

Hasty Generalization:
This is when a conclusion is drawn from a sample that is
too small or unrepresentative, leading to a conclusion
that is not logically justified by sufficient or unbiased
evidence.

Slippery Slope:
This occurs when someone claims that a position or
decision will lead to a series of unintended negative
consequences.

Straw Man:
This fallacy involves the deliberate distortion of another
person's argument. By oversimplifying or exaggerating
it, the other party creates an easy-to-refute argument and
then attacks it.

Vagueness Fallacy:
This fallacy occurs when an argument is made with terms
that are too vague or poorly defined, making it difficult
to assess the argument's validity or meaning. The lack of
precision prevents clear understanding and evaluation.